Terrace Talk

CW00664863

A Play for Wo

George MacEwan Green

Samuel French – London
New York – Sydney – Toronto – Hollywood

CHARACTERS

Madge, the parlour maid
Amy, the kitchen maid
Lady Harriet, the lady of the house
Julia, her daughter
Caroline, an old friend
Mavis, her daughter

The action of the play takes place on the terrace of a country house.

Time: a summer afternoon in an early year of the present century.

TERRACE TALK *

The terrace of a country house. At DSR and DSL are portions of a
stone balustrade. Back cloth of a portion of a house facade – ivy
wreathed windows. SC is a circular wrought–iron table, grouped
around this are basket chairs.
As the play opens MADGE is putting a crisp white cloth over the
table. AMY enters SR carrying a tray with a china tea service on
it. She wobbles precariously.

MADGE	(Noticing AMY.) For Gawd's sake, Amy girl, have a care. You're like a drunken sailor on Portsmouth High Street.
AMY	This thing's heavy, Madge.
MADGE	Stuff and nonsense! If you can carry the coals up to the drawing room – (winces as AMY bangs the tray down on the table) you can surely manage a few cups and saucers. (Picks up a cup and examines it.) Ooh, my sainted Auntie Kate, I think you've done for this one.
AMY	(hand to mouth) Oh no!
MADGE	Yes, girl, there's a distinct crack. (Looks at AMY and then giggles.) It's all right, it's only a hair. (Takes hair out and holds it up for inspection.)
AMY	You didn't half give me a fright. That's not

* N.B. Paragraph 3 on, page ii of this Acting Edition regarding
photocopying and video-recording should be carefully read.

nice, Madge.

MADGE	(Still holding hair.) Neither's this hair, if you ask me. Very black it is. Powerful black, in fact. Have you and that Irish groom been putting your heads together in the pantry again? (Lets hair flutter away.)
AMY	Give over. Him and me have got nothing in common.

(AMY and MADGE begin to arrange the tea set on the table.)

MADGE	Nothing in common, eh? You've had a nice time finding that out, the pair of you.
AMY	Don't know what you mean, Madge. Can't think where you get that idea from, I'm sure.
MADGE	From what I seen the two of you get up to behind the coach house last Thursday evening, that's where from, my girl.
AMY	Huh that! Why, we - we -
AMY & MADGE	Just happened to bump into one another!
MADGE	Well, have a care, Amy. I've done a fair bit of bumping into that Sean myself, girl, and I can tell you that what he's really after is a full-on collision.
AMY	I can send him off with a flea in his ear any time I want.
MADGE	And if you don't watch out for him he'll send you off, but it won't be with no flea and it certainly won't be in your ear neither. (Views table.) There, all properly laid.
AMY	(Picking up tray and looking wistfully at the table.) It must be nice to be them.
MADGE	Who?

AMY   <u>Them.</u> Coming out here and finding this
                       table all set out so pretty and just having to
                       sit down and start tucking in.

MADGE   Yes, well, there's more to it than that, of
                       course.

AMY   What more?

MADGE   There's - there's - well, there's the talk
                       for one thing.

AMY   Anyone can talk.

MADGE   Their kind of talk I mean. It's what's called
                       conversing. You wait until you've had some
                       more time in and you'll hear them at it your-
                       self. It's not easy, you know, conversing
                       isn't. It'd put a terrible strain on ordinary
                       folk's brains.

AMY   Whatever is it?

MADGE   It's politics and books and paintings and
                       things you'd never fathom out in a hundred
                       years. At last Friday's dinner party they
                       talked for two whole hours about the way
                       Prussians keep growing and expanding. Major
                       Dombleby-Foulkes didn't - he kept on about
                       giving raw eggs to Irish hunters - but Sir
                       John and Lady Harriet and all the others did.

AMY   (Plonking herself down in a chair and using
                       an affected voice.) Do be seated, Lady Madge.

MADGE   Here, you just watch it. We'd be packed off
                       bag and baggage if anyone spotted us.

AMY   Oh, go on! (MADGE reluctantly sits and
                       AMY resumes affected voice:) How naice of
                       you to call.

MADGE   (also with affected voice) A pleasure, I'm sure

                              Lady Amy.

AMY   Would you like to do a bit of conversing?

MADGE   I'd simply adore it. You start off, Lady
                              Amy, and I'll join in.

AMY   Yes, well, let me see. Isn't it queer the
                              way them Prussians keep growing?

MADGE   My word, yes, Lady Amy. They're growing
                              to a terrible height and expanding something
                              chronic.

AMY   They'll be hitting their heads on the ceiling
                              very soon, I shouldn't wonder, and them
                              spikes on their helmets will ruin the plaster,
                              mark my words.

MADGE   If you ask me, Lady Amy, I think they must
                              be knocking back a lot of raw eggs.

AMY   Like what Irish hunters do, Lady Madge?

MADGE   Yes, quaite. Your groom, Sean O'Reilly,
                              he's an Irish hunter isn't he not? Does he
                              go on the raw eggs?

AMY   Ho yes, but it don't make him no bigger -
                              (suddenly disolves into hee-haw laughter) -
                              leastways not as a respectable lady would
                              notice.

MADGE   (Laughing uproariously also.) But he doesn't
                              half expand round the back of a coach-house
                              of an evening.

LADY HARRIET   (off stage) Julia, it will be a perfectly splen-
                              did gown.

MADGE   My Gawd, Lady Harriet!

                              (MADGE and AMY leap to their feet, both

rubbing laughter tears from their eyes, AMY
still snorting. MADGE mimes to AMY that
she should make herself scarce. Still laughing AMY exits SR. MADGE stations herself
a little way back from the table. LADY
HARRIET enters SL followed by her daughter,
JULIA, who carries a book under her arm.
MADGE bobs a curtsy. LADY HARRIET sits
on a chair SR of table. JULIA sits on a chair
opposite. During their entrance they are
speaking:

JULIA   But everyone will know it's your chiffon
                        made over, Mamma.

LADY HARRIET   Of course they won't, Julia. Miss Pollywell,
                        in the village, is going to re-style it com-
                        pletely. She's quite a dexterous little woman.
                        She'll do a marvellous job. Once the sequins
                        have been removed –

JULIA   (interrupting) Removed! Oh Mamma, that's
                        wicked! The sequins are all that make the
                        wretched thing half tolerable.

LADY HARRIET   My darling girl, you're much too young for
                        sequins. You have the glitter of youth and
                        that's glitter enough for anyone. (to MADGE)
                        We are expecting Mrs Delaney and Miss
                        Mavis. Bring the tea five minutes after they
                        arrive.

MADGE   (Bobbing a curtsey.) Very good, m'lady.
                        (exits SR)

LADY HARRIET   I do wish, Julia, that you would not make
                        such a fuss over trivialities in front of the
                        servants. They expect a higher standard of
                        conduct than that and we are duty-bound not
                        to fail them in their expectations.

JULIA   I'm sorry, Mamma, but I did have my heart
                        set on a proper gown of my own for the

Willoughby's party.

LADY HARRIET	The party is little more than a soirée for older children and, anyway, the Willoughbys don't warrant the expense of a new dress.
JULIA	They're millionaires, Mamma!
LADY HARRIET	Only because they're industrialists glorified tin-smiths. Besides, there will be dresses enough when you do the London season. For the sake of that we must economize at present. Now do try to be sensible.
JULIA	Yes, Mamma. (Opens book and begins to read.)
LADY HARRIET	What are you reading?
JULIA	Swinburne.
LADY HARRIET	(vaguely) Swinburne? Is that entirely suitable, I wonder?
JULIA	It's poetry, Mamma.
LADY HARRIET	Then it's possibly harmless. It's prose one has to be so wary of. They put far too much reality into prose nowadays and it only serves to unsettle people. Books should be books and life should be life. The separateness of the two is the only thing which justifies the existence of literature.
JULIA	Yes, Mamma.
LADY HARRIET	(Consulting a fob watch.) I really did think the Delaneys would have arrived by now.
JULIA	For what time were they invited?
LADY HARRIET	They weren't. Mrs Delaney sent round a note to say that she and Mavis would like to

visit this afternoon. Evidently they were up
in town for a few days and newly returned
this morning. Doubtless they are agog with
some snippets of London gossip and are
under the delusion that we are equally agog
to be privy to them.

JULIA   I _like_ Mavis. I like her very much indeed.

LADY HARRIET   (surprised) You hardly need to sound so
                    defiant about it. She is, I agree, a pleasant,
                    unaffected child.

JULIA   But you don't care for Mrs Delaney, do you,
                    Mamma?

LADY HARRIET   Why, you've never heard me say such a
                    thing in your life!

JULIA   I know. I think, perhaps, that's why I have
                    the feeling that you may actually dislike her.

LADY HARRIET   Really, what a preposterous idea! And it's
                    entirely improper that you should speak to
                    me like this.

JULIA   I meant no disrespect, Mamma. I think if
                    one has some good reason for disliking some-
                    one, then one is perfectly justified in one's
                    dislike.

LADY HARRIET   My dear child, I don't dislike Mrs Delaney.
                    Since she is such a near neighbour I have
                    always made a point of being particularly
                    civil to her. And you know very well that
                    I've always made Mavis most welcome in
                    our family circle. There's absolutely no
                    question of dislike and so we'll say no more
                    on the subject.

JULIA   As you please, Mamma. (reads)

LADY HARRIET   There are some aspects of Mrs Delaney's

character I do not entirely admire, but I have never been anything but gracious to her.

JULIA

(looking up) Yes, Mamma. (reads)

LADY HARRIET

It's not always easy to be intimate with someone who has as forthright and honest a nature as Caroline Delaney.

JULIA

(looking up) But surely, Mamma, honesty and forthrightness are desirable virtues.

LADY HARRIET

No virtue is desirable if exhibited too often in public. I do not suggest that one should hide one's light under a bushel. On the other hand, there's no need to turn the bushel into a blazing torch.

JULIA

I have always considered Mrs Delaney to be a very modern sort of person.

LADY HARRIET

Everyone, Julia, is a modern sort of person. Only the dead may truly claim to be old fashioned. There is, however, such a thing as excessive modernity. It manifests itself as a desire to live through tomorrow before one has quite finished living through today. It is an excess indulged in by people of unstable temperament.

JULIA

Yes, Mamma. (reads)

LADY HARRIET

Your Pappa and poor Jack Delaney were tremendous chums and for the sake of that friendship I have very often gone out of my way to be courteous towards Caroline. I see her more often than any other friend I can think of.

JULIA

(Closes book.) Mavis adores her Pappa.

LADY HARRIET

But he was dead before she was even born.

JULIA   I mean, she adores his memory. Well, not
                     exactly his memory, for, of course, she
                     can't remember him. What she adores is
                     her mental vision of him. I rather admire
                     him as well. We think he must have been
                     very romantic to have died so young.

LADY HARRIET   There's nothing romantic about falling off a
                     horse. It ruined the season for the rest of
                     the hunt.

JULIA   But wasn't he marvellously wild and gay and
                     dashing?

LADY HARRIET   He was certainly frequently inebriated. Now,
                     you must not mention that to Mavis. It would
                     only be hurtful. And that is a good illustra-
                     tion of the desirability of reticence as opp-
                     osed to forthrightness.

JULIA   Yes, Mamma.

LADY HARRIET   Of course, dear Jack was something of a
                     charming rogue and everyone did adore him.
                     There's no denying that. He was what one
                     might call Byronic - not, thank heavens, that
                     I know anything whatsoever about Byron. At
                     the end of the day, however, it is reliability
                     and steadfastness that count for most.

JULIA   Like Pappa?

LADY HARRIET   Exactly. Your Pappa never had dash, but his
                     plod has taken him farther than Jack Delaney
                     could ever have gone. And he's never fallen
                     from a horse. At any rate, not from one in
                     motion..... Ah, our guests have arrived.

                     (CAROLINE and MAVIS DELANEY enter SL.
                     LADY HARRIET and JULIA rise and greet them
                     affectionately. MAVIS carries a small parcel.
                     After kissing one another MAVIS and JULIA
                     draw aside and appear to be whispering.)

CAROLINE   Harriet, I told your butler not to trouble
                   announcing us.

LADY HARRIET   Quite right, Caroline my dear. You need
                   stand on no ceremony in this house.

CAROLINE   I don't think your butler is quite as liberal
                   as you are, Harriet. I won't say he always
                   looks askance when I come barging into your
                   home, but he certainly keeps the corners of
                   his mouth as close to his chin as he possibly
                   can.

LADY HARRIET   You should know by now that Humbledon is
                   profoundly conservative. He likes to think
                   of the superior classes being kept on a tight
                   rein. He suspects that if they were ever
                   given their heads they would plunge blindly
                   into anarchy. But come, let us be seated.

                   (LADY HARRIET and CAROLINE sit.)

                   Girls, won't you seat yourselves?

                   (JULIA and MAVIS remain where they are.)

MAVIS   (Smiling broadly and speaking through
                   clenched teeth.) Do you notice anything
                   different about my appearance, Lady Harriet?

LADY HARRIET   (after a pause) Why no, Mavis dear. You
                   appear to be your usual pretty self.

JULIA   Oh, Mamma, can't you see? Mavis has had
                   her dental brace removed.

LADY HARRIET   Ah, of course. That's a great enhancement,
                   Mavis.

CAROLINE   I fear that until the novelty wears off I am to
                   be bereft of a daughter and to be saddled, in-
                   stead, with a ventriloquist's doll. Do stop
                   grinning so, my pet.

JULIA	I think she looks wonderfully sophisticated now.
MAVIS	Do you really, Julia?
JULIA	Absolutely.
CAROLINE	We saw the dentist when we were up in London and Mavis bullied the poor little man into declaring against his better judgement that her teeth are as even as modern science will ever make them.
LADY HARRIET	The dentist? I would have guessed from your chic appearance, Caroline, that it had been the couturière you visited in London.
CAROLINE	There also.
LADY HARRIET	Madame de la Roche?
CAROLINE	Yes. Do you like it?
LADY HARRIET	It's brilliantly à la mode.
CAROLINE	But you think it's much too ostentatious for the country.
LADY HARRIET	I assure you, no such thought entered my head.
CAROLINE	Then it should have. It is entirely too grandiose for the country and, indeed, for anywhere else either. And apart from being 'de trop' in style it was ridiculously 'de trop' in price as well. But there it was, lurking in Madame's showroom, ready to ambush just such a mad-woman as myself and I couldn't fight it off. No more could I resist wearing it as soon as we arrived home.
JULIA	If you ask me, Mrs Delaney, it's positively elegant.

LADY HARRIET   I don't think Mrs Delaney did ask you, Julia
                      darling.

CAROLINE   I rather wish I had.

LADY HARRIET   Now, girls, do come to the table. Tea will
                      be served presently.

JULIA   Mamma, Mavis and I should like to forego
                      tea. Mavis has brought something from
                      London she wishes to show to me.

LADY HARRIET   Is it so very urgent then?

CAROLINE   At their age everything is urgent.

MAVIS   (Holding up package.) I have brought a
                      phonograph recording.

LADY HARRIET   I see. Ah well, I suppose yours is a gener-
                      ation destined not to outgrow its toys. For-
                      sake us if you must then.

JULIA   We shall play it very quietly.

LADY HARRIET   We certainly hope so.

JULIA   Come along, Mavis. I can't wait to hear it.

                      (MAVIS and JULIA exit SL laughing.)

CAROLINE   They are much more at ease than we were at
                      their age.

LADY HARRIET   Whereas we, I feel, are infinitely less power-
                      ful than our mothers were. But you must tell
                      me all about town.

CAROLINE   It was wonderfully free of people; abysmally
                      free of gossip.

LADY HARRIET   You surprise me. Our weekend guests were
                      quite full of Lady Frippard's liason with

some Italian opera singer.

CAROLINE   Really? I heard nothing of the sort. Mind
                  you, I can well believe it. Lucy Frippard
                  has been widowed now for all of six weeks
                  and she never did let the grass grow very
                  long beneath her feet. I expect the grass
                  on Frippard's grave will fare no better than
                  any other.

LADY HARRIET   They do say –

                  (She breaks off sharply as MADGE and AMY
                  enter SR. MADGE carries a silver tray with
                  tea-pot etc. whilst AMY carries a cakestand
                  on which there are sandwiches, cherry cake
                  and gateaux.)

                  Sir Reginald was with us over the weekend.
                  He told us the Cabinet are regarding Prussian
                  growth and expansionist policies with some
                  disquiet.

CAROLINE   Hmm? Oh yes, but then I'm sure anything
                  which isn't actually fossilised into inertia
                  causes disquiet to our Cabinet.

                  (MADGE puts tray down in front of LADY
                  HARRIET. As she steps back she casts a
                  glance at AMY – obviously an 'I told you so'
                  inspired by LADY HARRIET's speech. Both
                  girls are afflicted with a suppressed fit of
                  the giggles which they contrive to disguise
                  as coughing.)

LADY HARRIET   For goodness sake, girls, don't splutter so
                  over everything.

                  (AMY places cakestand on table.)

LADY HARRIET   (to MADGE and AMY) You may go. And do
                  try to keep your germs in check.

14   TERRACE TALK

                          (MADGE and AMY bob curtsies and hands to
                          mouths, exit quickly SR. LADY HARRIET
                          pours tea and passes cup to CAROLINE.)

LADY HARRIET   They do say that the old Dowager Duchess
                          of Bolton has intervened.

CAROLINE   (amazed) Against Prussia?

LADY HARRIET   No, no, in the matter of Lucy Frippard's
                          liason. The duchess, they say, has left
                          Lucy in no doubt as to which side of a grand
                          piano a titled English widow should take her
                          stance in relation to a Neapolitan tenor.

                          (LADY HARRIET and CAROLINE sip their tea.)

CAROLINE   It is strange that you should mention the
                          Dowager Duchess. Thoughts of her crossed
                          my mind when I was sitting in McAllister's
                          waiting room.

LADY HARRIET   (surprised) Harley Street McAllister?

CAROLINE   Yes. There I was amidst that plethora of
                          shabby brown hide, clouds of carbolic and a
                          depressing excess of ancient Punch maga-
                          zines, my mind swarming with intimations
                          of mortality, when I suddenly realised that
                          I have gone through life without ever once
                          having been censured by the Dowager Duch-
                          ess of Bolton. I couldn't quite decide whe-
                          ther that was indicative of my having led an
                          astonishingly discreet life, or the fact that
                          Her Grace isn't nearly as astute as her
                          reputation would suggest.

LADY HARRIET   I trust your visit to McAllister was purely
                          routine.

CAROLINE   Certainly not. Anyone who would submit to
                          McAllister's obscene probings as a matter
                          of routine must have some kind of warped

character.

LADY HARRIET	Then you've been off colour? I had not realised.
CAROLINE	So much off colour that I dithered as to who I should consult first – McAllister or the sexton.
LADY HARRIET	I hope McAllister has now put your mind at rest.
CAROLINE	In a perverse sort of way he has. He told me, with a certain amount of grim, John Knoxian pleasure, that I shall be dead before the autumn is through.

(LADY HARRIET hestitates, teacup raised.)

LADY HARRIET	(quiet rebuke) You jest, of course, Caroline. (sips tea)
CAROLINE	Not at all, Harriet. Forgive the pun, but I am deadly serious.

(Slowly LADY HARRIET puts cup down on to saucer – it rattles a little.)

LADY HARRIET	You – you have not tried the cherry cake.
CAROLINE	I'm sorry, Harriet, I have embarrassed you.
LADY HARRIET	Good grief, no. That is (falters)
CAROLINE	It's terribly bad form, isn't it, to openly mention one's imminent death? I know it's de rigueur to suffer in silence, but the truth is that I felt I had to mention it to someone and since you are my closest friend –
LADY HARRIET	(interrupting) There's the chocolate gateau, as well.

CAROLINE

And now I've embarrassed you even more. It's even worse to tell someone she's your closest friend.

LADY HARRIET

I assure you, Caroline, I'm not embarrassed. It's just that -
(Again falters, then quietly, as if in response to something vaguely tiresome says:) Oh!

(LADY HARRIET rises abruptly and walks DSR to balustrade, standing with her back to CAROLINE. CAROLINE takes piece of cherry cake from stand and begins to nibble it.)

(Clearly controlling her emotion.) How can you speak of it so calmly?

CAROLINE

(with mouth full) This is really an excellent cherry cake, Harriet. (swallows) Calmly? I'll tell you. After hearing the verdict of that wild-eyed Scotsman I went back to my hotel room, my mind reeling with disbelief and outrage and goodness knows what other emotions. I stared at myself in the wardrobe mirror and then, very quietly, very systematically, I repeated the word 'death' until I was quite hoarse and quite reconciled to the sound of the word and to all its implications.

LADY HARRIET

I don't know what to say, Caroline.

CAROLINE

I'm glad. I mean, I'm glad you haven't gone plunging into a stream of platitudes. I could not bear cheering thoughts about 'life eternal' and reunions in Abraham's bosom. I've never cared for Abraham's bosom. It sounds so much as if one were about to have one's bones crushed in a monstrous bear-hug by a bumptious uncle in his nightshirt.

LADY HARRIET

(turning, half-laughing) Really, Caroline,

the things you say! (pauses, hoarsely) Oh, Caroline.

CAROLINE   (quietly) I know.

LADY HARRIET   Should you not be lying down?

CAROLINE   Harriet, I shall be permanently horizontal all too soon. I intend, therefore, to enjoy a vertical view of the world for as long as I may.

(JULIA enters SL)

JULIA   Mamma, Mavis has just taught me the steps of one of the very latest dances. We've taken the phonograph right up to the drawing-room window and now we're going to give you both a demonstration.

LADY HARRIET   Not just now, darling.

CAROLINE   Come, Harriet, a performance would be wonderful.

LADY HARRIET   Oh, very well.

JULIA   (shouts towards SL) Turn the machine on, Mavis.

MAVIS   (off) Right.

(Sounds of rag-time piano music. MAVIS comes dashing in from SL and she and JULIA go into a jerky hopping dance. LADY HARRIET returns to her seat, watches the dancers but her attention is really elsewhere. CAROLINE, however, is entranced and frequently laughs.)

CAROLINE   Isn't it splendid?

LADY HARRIET   What? Oh - I cannot believe it's supposed to be music. It sounds more like a cat leaping over the key-board.

CAROLINE	Exactly, my dear. Absolutely full of life.

(Music grinds to a deep-throated dirge and the dancers falter.)

MAVIS	Tcha, the machine has wound down.
JULIA	Did you like it, Mamma?
LADY HARRIET	It was hardly what I would call elegant.
CAROLINE	If you ask me, it's downright vulgar and I wish I were young enough to try it myself.
MAVIS	Has Mamma told you the deathly news, Lady Harriet?
LADY HARRIET	(extremely shocked) What?
MAVIS	That beastly Miss Pollywell has absolutely botched the dress she's making for me for the Willoughby's party.
LADY HARRIET	(with relief) No, Mavis, your Mamma has not yet got around to telling me that dreadful news.
CAROLINE	The child exaggerates. Miss Pollywell has only exercised some discretion regarding the styling of the neckline.
MAVIS	She's just ruined it, that's what she's done. She shouldn't be trusted with anything except children's clothes.
JULIA	With a bit of luck perhaps she'll botch my one entirely.
LADY HARRIET	Girls, we'll have no more defamation of poor Miss Pollywell's character. Go along and play some more with your infernal machine -

but do keep the window shut.

JULIA   All right, Mamma. Come along, Mavis.

                      (JULIA and MAVIS exit SL. LADY-HARRIET
                      rises and goes US, looking after them SL.)

LADY HARRIET   They're so fond of one another. Just like
                      sisters.

CAROLINE   Yes. (pauses - slight cough) But then they
                      are. I mean, they are sisters - at least,
                      half-sisters.

LADY HARRIET   (Turns to look at CAROLINE. Speaks in a
                      quite matter of fact voice:) Yes, I've
                      suspected that for some considerable time.

CAROLINE   And felt no hate for me?

LADY HARRIET   No, nothing quite so positive as hate; nothing
                      so excessive. Were you and John - ?

CAROLINE   In love? No, not in the least. Nothing so
                      excessive.

LADY HARRIET   I must have been carrying Julia at the time.

CAROLINE   Yes. That does make it seem particularly
                      wanton and beastly, doesn't it?

                      (LADY HARRIET comes back to table and sits.)

LADY HARRIET   More tea, Caroline?

CAROLINE   No thanks, Harriet. I suppose now is the
                      time to make a clean breast of it all, Will
                      you listen? (Pauses, then takes LADY HAR-
                      RIET's silence as a token of acquiescence.)
                      It was one afternoon in the summer. John
                      and Jack had both been up to London, and had
                      met on the train coming back here. Jack, as
                      usual, was terribly drunk. John saw him

home and he and I put Jack to bed. There
was a storm. I remember there was thunder
and lightning. The house was suddenly dark,
except for occasional flashes of white light.
I wasn't afraid - storms have never fright-
ened me - but I was depressed and my nerves
were on edge. I began to tell John everything
about the way things were between Jack and
myself. He felt sorry for me; momentarily
he pitied me. I, of course, pitied myself
dreadfully. He tried to comfort me and -
well, it just happened.

LADY HARRIET   I see.

CAROLINE   No one seduced anyone. We were both
                      seduced by the circumstances and, afterwards,
                      we were totally amazed that it should have
                      happened.

LADY HARRIET   A strange thing to have occurred whilst your
                      husband was in the house.

CAROLINE   He wasn't a husband, Harriet - not in the real
                      meaning of the word. Poor Jack's life was a
                      sham. All his gallantry and flirting was an
                      almighty pose. The truth was that women
                      scared him to death. He couldn't entirely
                      admit that - even to himself - and so he drank
                      to drown the truth. He never should have
                      married, but he did. He married me because -
                      oh, I don't know - because he thought I was a
                      good sport and because he thought I might
                      prove somehow different from the rest of the
                      female species.

LADY HARRIET   And you did rather - well, how shall I put it - ?

CAROLINE   Hound him? Yes, I did, didn't I? I was at the
                      silly age when one eschews bread and butter
                      for a diet of dreaming. It's not clever to
                      marry on an empty stomach and a light head.
                      Reality then strikes with all the force of acute

indigestion. Give Jack his due, he tried, as
they say, to do his duty, but it was frightful
for us both - frightful and grotesque and de-
void of all dignity.

LADY HARRIET   I'm sorry. In the absence of passion there
                      should, at least, be dignity. Of course,
                      everyone knew about Jack, but you are the
                      first person I've ever heard speak openly
                      about it.

CAROLINE   When I told John I was pregnant he was in a
                      dreadful tizzy. He was so afraid that I should
                      tell you the whole tale and that you'd be hurt.
                      You were his only real concern, Harriet,
                      believe me.

LADY HARRIET   I can believe you quite easily, Caroline.
                      John has always over-estimated my sensi-
                      tivity and I've always maintained my control
                      over him because of that.

CAROLINE   It is a benign and sensible control, Harriet.

LADY HARRIET   It is as much as he needs for his own good.
                      It must have been a relief to him that you
                      made no demands upon him.

CAROLINE   Most men would make abominable house-
                      keepers; they are most happy when dust is
                      swept under the carpets.

LADY HARRIET   And Jack?

CAROLINE   Quite undismayed. I rather believe he almost
                      convinced himself that it had happened at his
                      instigation.

LADY HARRIET   I'm glad I did not know anything of it at the
                      time. I was still a trifle immature. Never-
                      theless, I wish I had known of it before now.
                      I mean known for sure, instead of merely
                      having suspected something of the sort. You

might have found a better friend in me,
Caroline.

CAROLINE   Perhaps a more earnest friend, Harriet, but
                   probably not one half so stimulating. I've
                   rather enjoyed our see-saw relationship.
                   Now, I suppose what I really wish to do is -
                   dear God, it sounds so old fashioned - is to
                   commend my daughter to your care. I should
                   like to think that when I am dead -

LADY HARRIET   Mavis shall never be without a home and
                   never without a family whilst any of us live.

CAROLINE   I am content. Financially she will be amply
                   provided for -

LADY HARRIET   (interrupting) Please, Caroline.....

CAROLINE   Yes, of course, it's vulgar to talk about
                   money, isn't it?

LADY HARRIET   Dreadfully vulgar, Caroline. Except, of
                   course, when one is complaining about the
                   lack of it.

CAROLINE   There is one other vulgarity in which I wish
                   to indulge. I have decided that I really am
                   young enough to go into your drawing-room
                   and try to kick up my heels in that ludicrous
                   dance. You promise, however, Harriet, that
                   you won't scowl me into shame.

LADY HARRIET   You may do as you please, Caroline, as long
                   as you don't try to inveigle me into doing any-
                   thing ridiculous as well.

                   (They rise and walk SL)

                   By the way, Julia was perfectly correct -
                   your outfit is positively elegant.

CAROLINE   Why, thank you.

LADY HARRIET	You, also, were correct, Caroline; it really isn't suitable for the country.
CAROLINE	Dear Harriet.

(They hesitate, kiss lightly on the cheek and exit SL. There is a pause, then MADGE and AMY enter SR. They carry trays on to which they load the various tea-things:)

MADGE	Mr Humbledon said as how she could go up to her room until she'd calmed herself.
AMY	Who? Beth?
MADGE	Yes. Ooh, she was in a state. Terrible worked up she was, poor soul. She's had a letter, you see.
AMY	It's got to do with her mother or something, hasn't it?
MADGE	Um.... her Pa died, you know – an accident in the quarry – and the company put her Ma out of the cottage. Now she's ended up in the charity ward with this thing what's killing her.
AMY	What thing?

(MADGE mouths her reply.)

(perplexed) Huh?

MADGE	(loudly, impatiently) A growth!

(There is a rather embarrassed pause, because both girls know they have crossed a taboo line.)

AMY	Poor Beth.
MADGE	(briskly) Yes. Well, that's life.

AMY	I suppose - but it makes you think, don't it.
MADGE	No, it don't, girl, for it don't bear thinking on.
AMY	It's funny, 'nt it, the way we was going on about them Prussians and their -
MADGE	(interrupting) That's a different kind of growth, you fool.
AMY	I know! But it's the idea - it's the frighten-ingness of it what's the same.
MADGE	Stuff and nonsense. You finished?
AMY	Yes. (giggles) Here, what do you think of that Robinson, the Delaney's coachman?
MADGE	Greedy-guts he is. Did you see the way he polished off them scones what cook give him with his tea? Like feeding buns to one of them helephants at the zoo.
AMY	It don't show though, do it? He hasn't gone to fat, has he now?
MADGE	Must work it off somehow.
	(Both girls start giggling.)
AMY	Warrant you wouldn't mind helping him with that kind of work.
MADGE	I might. But I tell you, he'd be the one as would end up wearing the harness and the blinkers.
AMY	Ooh, hark at you! Giddy-up Robinson! Come on, keep your tail up boy!
MADGE	Ssh!
AMY	What?

MADGE   Listen!

                         (off faint sounds of gramaphone music and
                         distant laughter.)

MADGE   High-jinks in the drawing-room.

AMY   (wistfully) That's the life and no mistake.
                         Not a worry, not a care.

                         (The two girls walk SR to exit:)

                         How about having a chat with him?

MADGE   With Robinson? Wouldn't know where to start.

AMY   Ask him what he thinks of them there
                         Prussians.

MADGE   He'd probably know more about raw eggs and
                         Irish hunters.

AMY   Either way it'd be a start. Take care of the
                         start and the end will take care of itself.
                         Come on, let's have some fun while we can.

                         (They exit SR. The music continues then
                         dwindles away and there is a slow fade.)

                         CURTAIN

MADE AND PRINTED IN GREAT BRITAIN BY
LATIMER TREND & COMPANY LTD, PLYMOUTH
MADE IN ENGLAND